SALMA HAYEK

A Real-Life Reader Biography

Valerie Menard

Mitchell Lane Publishers, Inc.
P.O. Box 200 • Childs, Maryland 21916

First Printing

Real-Life Reader Biographies

Selena	Robert Rodriguez	Mariah Carey	Rafael Palmeiro
Tommy Nuñez	Trent Dimas	Cristina Saralegui	Andres Galarraga
Oscar De La Hoya	Gloria Estefan	Jimmy Smits	Mary Joe Fernandez
Cesar Chavez	Chuck Norris	Sinbad	Paula Abdul
Vanessa Williams	Celine Dion	Mia Hamm	Sammy Sosa
Brandy	Michelle Kwan	Rosie O'Donnell	Shania Twain
Garth Brooks	Jeff Gordon	Mark McGwire	**Salma Hayek**
Sheila E.	Hollywood Hogan	Ricky Martin	Britney Spears
Arnold Schwarzenegger			

Library of Congress Cataloging-in-Publication Data
Menard, Valerie.
    Salma Hayek / Valerie Menard.
        p. cm. — (A real-life reader biography)
    Includes index.
    Summary: A biography of the Mexican-born actress who started her career on television and went on to star in "Fools Rush In" and other films.
    ISBN 1-58415-018-1
    1. Hayek, Salma, 1968- Juvenile literature. 2. Actors—Mexico Biography Juvenile literature. [1. Hayek, Salma. 1968- . 2. Actors and actresses. 3. Women Biography.] I. Title. II. Series.
PN2318.H39M46 1999
791.43'028'092—dc21
[B]
                                                    99-29471
                                                      CIP

ABOUT THE AUTHOR: Valerie Menard has been an editor for *Hispanic* magazine since the magazine moved to Austin, Texas, in July 1994. Before joining the magazine, she was a managing editor of a bilingual weekly, *La Prensa*. Valerie writes from a Latino perspective and as an advocate for Latino causes. She is the author of several biographies for children including **Oscar De La Hoya** and **Cristina Saralegui**.

PHOTO CREDITS: cover: Shooting Star; p. 4 Ron Davis/Shooting Star; p. 16 Fitzroy Barrett/Globe Photos; p. 17 The Kobal Collection; p. 19 Reuters/Mike Segar/Archive Photos; p. 22 Kobal Collection; p. 24 Lisa Rose/Globe Photos; p. 28 Archive Photos; p. 30 Kobal Collection

ACKNOWLEDGMENTS: The following story has been thoroughly researched, and to the best of our knowledge, represents a true story. Though we try to authorize every biography that we publish, for various reasons, this is not always possible. This story is neither authorized nor endorsed by Salma Hayek or any of her representatives.

Table of Contents

Chapter 1   A Mexican Childhood 5

Chapter 2   A Prankster Becomes an Actress 9

Chapter 3   Salma's American Dream 13

Chapter 4   A Starring Role 20

Chapter 5   The Actress Matures 25

Filmography   31

Chronology 32

Index 32

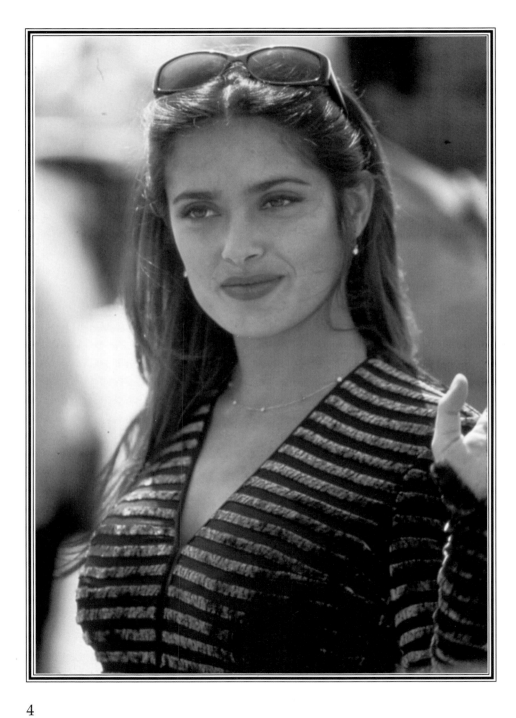

Chapter 1
A Mexican Childhood

When Salma Hayek was a little girl growing up in Mexico, she used to dream about becoming a movie actress. Sometimes, when she went to the movies, she pretended she was on the screen. As she grew up, her desire to act became stronger. With her great beauty, some talent, and a little luck, Salma set out to make her dreams come true.

Salma Hayek Jimenez was born on September 2, 1968. Her parents, Sami and Diana, lived in the small town of Coatzacoalcos, which is located in the Mexican state of Veracruz. Salma's

When Salma Hayek was a little girl, she used to dream about becoming a movie actress.

father is Lebanese, although he was born and raised in Mexico. He worked at a local oil company. Salma's mother is of Spanish ancestry and was born in Mexico. After Salma was born, Sami and Diana had a son. They named him Sami Jr.

When Salma was young, her mother taught her an important lesson: you can succeed at anything if you work hard. Diana liked to sing and dreamed of becoming an opera singer. One day, she announced to the family that she was going to pursue a singing career. She trained her voice and practiced constantly. She even stopped talking to her children—Diana would sing to them instead! "We'd come to her and say, 'Can we got to the movies?' and she would sing, 'Wha-a-at mo-o-ovie are you going to-o-o?'" Salma remembered in an August 1998 *In Style* magazine article.

All Diana's hard work paid off. She began to get singing jobs. Eventually,

> **Salma's mother is of Spanish ancestry and was born in Mexico.**

she opened a school to teach young people how to sing.

In Coatzacoalcos, oil was a major industry. When Salma was growing up, the Mexican government owned the only oil company, Petroleos de México (PEMEX). The oil company was a big employer in Salma's home town. Because her father had a good job with PEMEX, Salma and her family lived comfortably. She remembers a childhood filled with fun things like studying gymnastics, drinking coconut milkshakes, and eating sweet pork tacos. When Salma was little, her grandmother, Maria Louisa Lopez, had an odd ritual. She would shave Salma's head and trim her eyebrows so that they would grow back thicker.

But although the oil company's operation in Coatzacoalcos made these nice memories possible for Salma's family, there was a downside as well. Sometimes oil spills polluted the local beach, and the air often smelled bad

Salma remembers a childhood filled with fun things like studying gymnastics, drinking coconut milkshakes, and eating sweet pork tacos.

Salma spent much of her free time at the movies.

because of fumes that were released by the refinery. Many children pretended that they were in a better place, and Salma was no different. She would spend as much time as she could at the movies. Her favorite day was Sunday, when she and her father went to afternoon shows together. Inside the movie theater, it was cool and dark, and Salma could let her imagination run wild. The more movies she watched, the more she wished that someday she could become an actress. At the end of each movie, she would even close her eyes and imagine seeing her name in the credits.

Chapter 2
A Prankster Becomes an Actress

Salma knew it was important to get a good education. Her parents also knew the value of school. They decided to send her to the United States to finish her education. She attended a Roman Catholic boarding school in Louisiana called the Academy of the Sacred Hearts.

Salma was a practical joker in school. She told *GQ* magazine that one time, during study hour, she asked to go to the bathroom. Instead, she snuck into the buildings where the students lived and set all the clocks back three hours. Even though she got in trouble for her

An education was important to Salma and her parents.

pranks, Salma was also a good student. She graduated from high school when she was just 16.

After she finished school in the United States, she returned to Mexico. She was still young and trying to find herself. For a while, she listened to punk rock music and wore ripped T-shirts, studded collars, and spiked hair. Then, she dropped this wild look and started dressing in suits, skirts, and oversized sweaters. Eventually, Salma enrolled in the Universidad Iberamericana in Mexico City. She studied international relations and drama. However, what Salma really wanted was to be an actress. So she left school to take acting classes full time and audition for roles.

It was difficult at first. Many people want to act, and Salma was always competing for parts. In 1989, she got her first big break. Salma had a role in a production of the play *Aladdin*. During the play, she was noticed by a man who made television programs. He

After she graduated from high school in the United States, Salma returned to Mexico.

was one of the most important producers of *telenovelas*, the Mexican equivalent of American soap operas.

Telenovelas are different from soap operas in several ways. The most important difference is that they end. The telenovelas can be canceled at any time, but even the most popular ones usually end after four months. Because of this, the plots can be very outrageous.

The telenovelas producer hired Salma for her first television acting job on his show *Nuevo Amanecer.* This role led to others. Salma took a big step when she won the title role in the telenovela *Teresa.* As Teresa, she played a social climber who could be very mean, but because the audience was supposed to like Teresa, Salma had to act really sweet as well. Salma soon became very famous, and she won Mexico's equivalent of an Emmy Award.

When *Teresa* ended, Salma continued to get work on different shows. She remained very popular with

In 1989, Salma got her big break when she captured a role in a Mexican soap opera.

In 1991, Salma decided to try to make a career in Hollywood.

television viewers. Many telenovelas are also broadcast in the United States, on Spanish television networks like Univision and Telemundo, so she began to develop fans in the U.S. as well.

In 1991, Salma decided she didn't want to be a soap opera actress. Even though she had a successful career, she packed her things and moved to Hollywood. "I didn't want to act in soap operas the rest of my life," she told a reporter for *Time International.* "I don't even watch them. I wasn't interested in social position but in artistic integrity."

Even though it was hard for Latina actors to find work in Hollywood, Salma Hayak was committed to her dream of becoming a movie star.

Chapter 3
Salma's
American Dream

Salma came to Hollywood with all the confidence in the world. She had already begun a successful television acting career in Mexico and she had attended school in the United States. She was certain that she would be able to audition for English-speaking movie roles.

However, Salma overestimated her language skills. She soon realized that she needed to go back to school and work on her English. She enrolled in the Stella Adler School, where she studied the plays and poetry of William Shakespeare. Salma would continue to

Even though she had been educated in the United States, she still had to work on her English.

Soon, Salma landed some small parts on TV.

take classes for two years, and to this day, still works with a voice coach.

In the meantime, she was able to find some work. In 1992 she landed a guest spot on the HBO comedy series *Dream On*, and the next year, she appeared on the NBC series *Nurses*. In 1993, she also earned a regular role on Fox-TV's *The Sinbad Show*. The show starred African-American comedian Sinbad as a computer programmer who was raising two children. She played Sinbad's neighbor Gloria. The show was soon canceled.

Salma thought her telenovela acting experience would not help in Hollywood, but it would eventually lead to her first movie role. Because she was a famous telenovela actress, she appeared on several Spanish-language talk shows. While flipping through the television channels one night in 1993, a Hispanic movie director named Robert Rodriguez paused to watch Salma being interviewed on comedian Paul Rodriguez's talk show. Robert knew right away that he wanted to cast Salma in his next movie.

Robert Rodriguez had made his first movie, *El Mariachi*, for $7,000. It was the story of a Mexican musician who is accidentally mistaken for a hit man and gets involved with some gangsters. They kill his lover and mutilate his hand, so that he can not play the guitar well anymore. The movie was a surprise hit at the Sundance Film Festival, where it won the Audience Award. Because of this success, *El Mariachi* was released in theaters and became popular. Rodriguez was also asked to make another movie with a bigger budget. He decided this film, *Desperado*, would be a sequel to *El Mariachi*. It would follow the adventures of the young guitar player as he set out for revenge. Along the way, he falls in love with a beautiful young woman who owns a bookstore. Together, they help rid the town of the bad guy.

Rodriguez had already selected a Spanish actor named Antonio Banderas

Film director Robert Rodriguez wanted to cast Salma in his new movie, *Desperado*.

for the lead role. He thought that Salma would be perfect as the bookstore owner, Carolina. However, Salma was an unknown Mexican actress. Studio executives wanted him to hire someone famous for the part.

Salma with good friend, film director Robert Rodriguez

To prove how good Salma could be, Rodriguez cast her in another movie he was making, called *Roadracers*. This one was created for the cable channel Showtime in 1994. Once the movie studio executives saw her in *Roadracers*, they agreed to let Rodriguez hire her for *Desperado*.

When *Desperado* was

released in 1995, it instantly made a star of Antonio Banderas. Salma Hayak also received praise for her part in the movie. *Desperado* turned out to be very popular.

While Desperado was getting Salma noticed in the United States, a movie that she had done in Mexico the

Salma with actor Antonio Banderas during the filming of Desperado

year before was becoming a big hit. She had a serious dramatic part in the Mexican film *El Callejon de los Milagros* (Miracle Alley). For her part, she was nominated for Mexico's highest film award, the Ariel, as best actress. Although she didn't win, the film won the 1995 Ariel for best picture.

Before the year ended Robert Rodriguez gave Salma a small part in another movie, *Four Rooms*. The movie was actually made up of four short movies by different directors. Robert Rodriguez directed the segment with Salma, called "The Misbehavers." The next year, Rodriguez gave her another substantial role in his film *From Dusk Till Dawn*. The movie starred George Clooney, who was one of the hottest actors at the time, as well as Quentin Tarantino, who was making his acting debut after directing hit films like *Reservoir Dogs* and *Pulp Fiction*. They played brothers who escape to Mexico after a bank robbery. However, the bar where they have decided to meet is filled with vampires, and they have to stay alive through the night. Salma played one of the vampires, and the popularity of the film increased interest in her career.

She followed up by starring in another movie in 1996, *Fled*. Salma played a woman who helps two escaped convicts on the run from police. The prisoners were played by Laurence Fishburne and Stephen Baldwin, both big-name stars.

Salma was on her way in Hollywood.

Salma arrived at New York's Metropolitan Museum of Art for the Costume Institute Gala to introduce the Gianni Versace Exhibition on December 8, 1997.

Chapter 4
A Starring Role

In 1997, Salma starred in the box office hit *Fools Rush In.*

In 1997, Salma Hayek scored her first starring role in *Fools Rush In*, a romantic comedy. She co-starred with Matthew Perry, one of the stars of the television show *Friends*. In the movie, she plays a Latina named Isabel Fuentes who has a one-night stand with a young New York businessman and becomes pregnant. They decided to get married. However, because her husband, played by Perry, is not Latino, some of their problems grow from not understanding each other's culture.

This was a very important movie for Salma because as one of the stars she could offer the director insights about her character. According to the director of *Fools Rush In*, Andy Tennant, Salma had a lot of good suggestions. "This movie lives or dies by Salma Hayek," explained Tennant.

One of Salma's suggestions was adding a scene where Isabel discusses her pregnancy with her mother while they are lighting candles in church. According to Salma, any Roman Catholic Mexican woman would talk about such an important issue with her mother. "What Salma brings to the part is production smarts," Tennant tells *Time International* reporter Laura Lopez. "She's not just concerned with herself and her role but with the whole production. She looks at material like a studio executive, which is rare."

Salma earned $500,000 for this movie, a very good salary. However, there was another reason *Fools Rush In* was so important to her career. In *Desperado* and many of her other movies, Salma had played beautiful and

Salma was able to contribute to the movie in other ways, as well.

sexy characters. In *Fools Rush In*, Salma's character was struggling with real problems. For an actress, especially one as pretty and smart as Salma, it's important to move away from playing just one type of character. "I'm a woman, a Latina, and I have a sexy reputation," explains Salma. "This industry is run by men who are surprised that you could come up with a

Salma starred with Matthew Perry in the film Fools Rush In.

good idea, and even if they think it's good, they say 'no.'"

Salma always kept her sense of humor, which helped her deal with the challenge of developing as an actress in Hollywood. "Every time [reporters would] talk about me, they'd use some strange word I'd never heard before [like] 'Bombshell.' What does that mean? I'm reading this and thinking I bombed the movie," she joked to one interviewer.

After *Fools Rush In*, Salma appeared in a movie about nightclub life in the 1970s called *54*, and in another Rodriguez movie, *The Faculty*. She also starred in an independent film, *Breaking Up*, with Russell Crowe, and took the part of Esmeralda in a television movie version of *The Hunchback of Notre Dame*. She may have gotten this part because she provided the voice for Esmeralda in the Spanish-language version of Disney's cartoon version of *The Hunchback of Notre Dame*. While Salma was making *Hunchback* for the cable

Salma has been able to keep her sense of humor while trying to make a career in Hollywood.

television network TNT, she met the British actor Edward Atterton. They started dating, and have been together since then. Salma also invited her little brother, Sami, to live with her in Los Angeles, where he works as an environmental designer.

Chapter 5
The Actress Matures

As Salma Hayek discovered, it is difficult for Latino actors and actresses to find jobs in Hollywood. Many movies do not feature Latino characters. Even when they do, Latino actors don't always get hired for those roles. For example, in the 1950s American actor Marlon Brando played the title role in a film about the Mexican revolutionary Emiliano Zapata. More recently, British actor Sir Anthony Hopkins took two roles—Spanish painter Pablo Picasso and the aging Zorro character in the 1998 film *Zorro*—that could have been played by a Latino. It was even harder

It is difficult for Latino actors and actresses to find jobs in Hollywood.

for Latinas in Hollywood. No Mexican actress had achieved superstar status since the famous Dolores Del Rio achieved success in the 1930s.

In 1990, a movie studio decided to make a film about the famous Mexican painter Frida Kahlo. The story of Kahlo is so interesting that a lot of actresses wanted to play her in the film. Even pop stars like Madonna wanted the role. Director Luis Valdez was under pressure to cast a famous actress, rather than a Latina. He chose Laura San Giacomo. She was not a Latina but had just been noticed for her work in *Sex, Lies and Videotape.* However, when many Hispanics loudly protested the choice of San Giacomo, the project was put on hold.

Almost ten years later, plans to make the movie came up again. But this time there was no question who would play the title role of Kahlo in the film *Frida*—Salma Hayek. This was a big step forward for Latinas. A Mexican actress

Movie studios often make films about Latinos and use non-Latino actors and actresses.

with the appeal and popularity to carry a project was not only being cast in a lead role, but would actually get to portray a famous historical Mexican character!

"I auditioned a year and a half or two years ago," Salma remembered in an *In Style* interview. "When I first auditioned, they said that they didn't want to do it with a non-Mexican, but they didn't think any Mexican actress had a big enough name to do it."

However, in the time after her first audition, Salma became famous. She also opened her own production company, Ventanarosa (rose window). A production company is very important because it means actors don't have to depend on a Hollywood studio for work. Instead, they can choose which movie they want to be in so long as they can find the money to make it. When she was asked to do the part of Kahlo, Salma insisted on producing the film as

In 1998, Salma started her own production company.

well. "I believe things happen for a reason," she says.

Like her mother, Salma wants to help Mexican children participate in the arts. This kind of a project needs money, so Salma plans to donate her profits from *Frida* to fund scholarships for students to attend art school. She hopes to start a foundation named after Kahlo,

In January 1999, Salma attended the White House State dinner for Argentine President Carlos Menem.

to help promote the arts to children in Mexico.

While she was working on *Frida*, Salma kept busy with other projects as well. Her 1999 movies include *Dogma*, in which she co-stars with Matt Damon; *The Velocity of Gary* with Vincent D'Onforio; and *The Wild Wild West* with Will Smith. She's also a spokesperson for Revlon cosmetics. Her future plans include returning to Mexico to film a television movie based on the book by Colombian author Gabriel Garcia Marquez, *El Coronel no Tiene Quien le Escriba (The Colonel Has No One to Write To)*.

Although Salma Hayek left Mexico to find success in Hollywood, her heart and soul are still there. With her face in magazines, on television, and in the movies, the actress is an inspiration to many young Hispanics. "My way of defending Latinos is by working and showing that we're just as good," she explained in an interview. "I hope that I

Salma's heart and soul are still in Mexico.

Salma is one of the few Latinas able to make a living in Hollywood.

am an inspiration for anyone who has been told, 'No, you can't do that,' and was laughed at for having a dream." Salma Hayek is proof positive that with hard work and determination, dreams do come true.

Filmography

1993 *Mi Vida Loca* (My Crazy Life)
1994 *El Callejon De Los Milagros* (Miracle Alley)
1995 *Desperado*
1995 *Four Rooms*
1995 *Fair Game*
1996 *From Dusk Till Dawn*
1996 *Disney's The Hunchback of Notre Dame* (voice over)
1996 *Fled*
1997 *Fools Rush In*
1997 *54*
1997 *Breaking Away*
1999 *Frida*
1999 *Dogma*
1999 *The Velocity of Gary*
1999 *The Wild Wild West*

Television movies

1994 *Road Racers* (Showtime)
1996 *The Hunchback* (TNT)

Chronology

1968   Salma Hayek is born in Coatzacoalcos, Veracruz, Mexico, on September 2.

1984   Graduates from high school at age 16

1987   Attends the Universidad Iberamericana to study international relations and drama.

1989   Cast in the lead role in *Teresa*, a Spanish-language telenovela.

1991   Leaves her successful acting career in Mexico to try Hollywood

1993   Makes first movie appearance, in *Mi Vida Loca* (My Crazy Life)

1995   Cast in her first major Hollywood picture, *Desperado*; nominated for Ariel Award for *El Callejon de los Milagros*

1996   Appears in *From Dusk Till Dawn* and *Fled*; meets her boyfriend Edward Atterton while making the television movie, *The Hunchback of Notre Dame*.

1997   Stars with Matthew Perry in the romantic comedy *Fools Rush In*.

1998   Starts her own production company, Ventanarosa

1999   Wins the title role in the movie *Frida*; stars with Will Smith in *The Wild Wild West*.

Index

Academy of the Sacred Hearts 9

Aladdin 10

Atterton, Edward 24

Baldwin, Stephen 19

Banderas, Antonio 17

Brando, Marlon 25

Clooney, George 18

Del Rio, Dolores 26

Desperado 15, 16, 17

Dream On 14

Fishburne, Laurence 19

Fools Rush In 20–22

From Dusk Till Dawn 18

Hayek, Salma
    birth of 5

brother 6, 24

charity 28

education of 9–10

goes to Hollywood 12

parents of 5–7

Hayek, Sami (father) 5–6

Jimenez, Diana (mother) 6–7

Kahlo, Frida 26, 27, 28

Lopez, Maria (grandmother) 7

Perry, Matthew 20

Rodriguez, Paul 14

Rodriguez, Robert 14–18

telenovelas 11–12

Tennant, Andy 21

Valdez, Luis 26